How to Write
Writing in a Journal

by Nick Rebman

FOCUS READERS®
BEACON

www.focusreaders.com

Copyright © 2024 by Focus Readers®, Mendota Heights, MN 55120. All rights reserved. No part of this book may be reproduced or utilized in any form or by any means without written permission from the publisher.

Focus Readers is distributed by North Star Editions:
sales@northstareditions.com | 888-417-0195

Produced for Focus Readers by Red Line Editorial.

Photographs ©: Shutterstock Images, cover, 1, 4, 7, 11, 16, 21, 22, 25; iStockphoto, 8, 13, 14–15, 18, 29; Red Line Editorial, 26–27

Library of Congress Cataloging-in-Publication Data
Library of Congress Cataloging-in-Publication Data is available on the Library of Congress website.

ISBN
979-8-88998-027-8 (hardcover)
979-8-88998-070-4 (paperback)
979-8-88998-153-4 (ebook pdf)
979-8-88998-113-8 (hosted ebook)

Printed in the United States of America
Mankato, MN
012024

About the Author

Nick Rebman is a writer and editor who lives in Minnesota.

Table of Contents

CHAPTER 1
Hard Day 5

CHAPTER 2
Getting Started 9

Trust Yourself 14

CHAPTER 3
Free Writing 17

CHAPTER 4
Many Possibilities 23

Focus on Writing in a Journal • 28

Glossary • 30

To Learn More • 31

Index • 32

Chapter 1

Hard Day

A girl walks home from school. She had a hard day. She argued with her best friend. The girl gets home and grabs her favorite pen. Then she sits down in her favorite spot.

 Strong feelings can be hard to handle. Naming them can be a first step. Some are happy, sad, angry, and afraid.

The girl opens her journal. She starts writing about what happened at school. She explains what her friend said. She also describes how those words made her feel.

The girl is glad that she wrote about the fight. It helped her understand her own feelings. It

Did You Know?

Some problems feel too big to talk about. Writing in a journal can help. You can start to **process** your feelings.

 Struggles in friendships happen. Repairing them can make the friendship feel stronger than before.

also helped her understand why her friend got mad. The next day, she talks to her friend. Before long, the friendship feels repaired.

Chapter 2

Getting Started

The purpose of a journal is to keep a record of your thoughts and feelings. There is no wrong way to do it. Many people write their journals in notebooks. Others prefer to write on computers.

 Writing by hand uses the body to slowly form words. For some people, that helps with processing.

Try to keep a regular schedule with your journal. Some people write every day. But it doesn't have to be that often. You might decide to write once or twice a week.

Writing in a journal should not feel like work. So, don't worry about writing a certain amount. Some days, your entry might be short. Other days, it will be long.

Every time you begin a new entry, write the date. Then, write about whatever you're thinking about

 Some people like to be outside when they write. Others prefer to be inside.

that day. Sometimes you'll write about happy things. Other times, you'll write about sad things. Both are okay.

You can also write about things you're interested in. Or you can explain what you're afraid of. Memories are another great topic. So are plans for the future.

Journals can also help you make decisions. Suppose your friend invites you to a movie next

Did You Know?

Some people write each journal entry like it's a letter. For example, an entry might start with "Dear Diary."

> You can't always know the results of a choice. But writing can help you think about likely results.

weekend. But you already have plans with your grandpa. You can make a list in your journal. How will each person feel if you don't join them? How will you feel?

WRITE LIKE A PRO

Trust Yourself

Sometimes it can be scary to tell others what you're thinking. But your thoughts are important. So, don't be afraid to write them down. You can keep your journal **private**. No one else has to see what you write.

Maybe you're afraid of swimming. Being afraid is normal. But it might feel **embarrassing**. Writing in a journal can help. First, explain how being in the water makes you feel. Then, explain why. Over time, you may find it easier to deal with your fears.

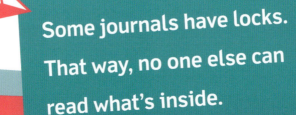

Some journals have locks. That way, no one else can read what's inside.

Chapter 3

Free Writing

Spelling and **grammar** are important in most kinds of writing. But in journaling, the rules don't matter. You can do whatever feels right. Use any style that helps you get your thoughts down.

 Some journals are very colorful. Other journals are simple.

17

 Using paintbrushes can help express things that might feel harder with pen or pencil.

Journaling is also a good way to experiment. For example, you can try new styles of writing. Give new words a try, too. One day, you might use short sentences and simple words. Another day, you might use long sentences and big words. Some days, you might not use sentences at all. The entries can be more like poetry.

Suppose you went on a vacation. Your journal entry might use realistic language. Then, you can describe every detail of the trip.

Some people like to add drawings or photos to their journals. Others add stickers or stamps.

Remember to use all five senses. Capture the sights, sounds, smells, tastes, and feel of the place you visited.

Later on, your entry might focus more on how you're feeling. To do that, you might use **similes** and **metaphors**. This type of language isn't realistic. Instead, it can help show your emotions. For example, suppose you took first place in a race. You might want to capture how it felt to win. You may write, "I

 The simile "I ran like a bolt of lightning" connects lightning's speed to your speed.

ran like a bolt of lightning. When I won, I was so happy that I felt like I was floating."

Chapter 4

Many Possibilities

Some days, you might not know what to write about. **Prompts** can help. Make a list of topics. For example, imagine places you'd like to visit. Or describe things you'd like to do when you're older.

 If you think of many new ideas to write about, you can save some for later.

There are many ways to journal. That's why some people have more than one journal. Each one can be about a certain topic. One journal might be about dreams you've had. Another could be about the movies you've seen. And another could focus on your favorite hobby.

Did You Know?

If you're not sure what to write about, try looking up prompts online. You can find many questions or ideas to get you started.

> **Having more than one journal can help organize your thoughts, experiences, and interests.**

Journals capture your feelings at a specific time. So, look back at old entries once in a while. Think about how you felt on those days. Have you learned anything since then?

Would you feel differently if the same thing happened today?

Journaling has many benefits. It can help you remember events. And it can improve your writing. Each time you write, you'll get practice describing people, places, or feelings.

Journaling can help you be more creative, too. Also, it can improve your **mental health**. Writing about your life is a great way to deal with stress.

PARTS OF A JOURNAL

07/24/23 — date

letter entry — Dear Diary,

I'M STUMPED!

writing prompt — Yesterday, my class did storm clouds and rainbows. Each shared a hard thing (🌧️) and a nice thing (🌈). I will do that today.

🌧️ I had a bad dream. I was running, but I could not escape. I felt scared.

🌈 I asked Frankie to be my friend, and he said yes. 🙂

drawing

27

FOCUS ON
Writing in a Journal

Write your answers on a separate piece of paper.

1. Write a paragraph that explains the main ideas of Chapter 3.

2. Would you prefer to write a journal in a notebook or on a computer? Why?

3. What should every journal entry include?
   - **A.** the date
   - **B.** a happy memory
   - **C.** a metaphor

4. When are prompts most useful?
   - **A.** when you just got back from a fun vacation
   - **B.** when you got into an argument with your friend
   - **C.** when you can't think of anything to write about

5. What does **schedule** mean in this book?

*Try to keep a regular **schedule** with your journal. Some people write every day. But it doesn't have to be that often.*

    A. a person who is good at writing
    B. a plan for doing something at a specific time
    C. a book that includes thoughts and feelings

6. What does **experiment** mean in this book?

*Journaling is also a good way to **experiment**. For example, you can try new styles of writing.*

    A. to try something different
    B. to avoid writing for many days
    C. to think about your favorite writers

Answer key on page 32.

Glossary

embarrassing
Causing a feeling of shame, nervousness, or self-doubt.

grammar
The rules of language, including the forms of words and how to order words in sentences.

mental health
How well or unwell someone's mind is, including their emotions and thinking.

metaphors
Words that describe something by referring to it as another thing. For instance, a person who stays up late might be called a "night owl."

private
Not shared with others.

process
To think about something in order to better understand it.

prompts
Topics that people use to guide their writing.

similes
Words that describe something by comparing it to another thing, using "like" or "as." For instance, a person who always stays active might be called "as busy as a bee."

To Learn More

BOOKS

Eason, Sarah, and Louise Spilsbury. *How Do I Write Well?* Shrewsbury, UK: Cheriton Children's Books, 2022.

Heinrichs, Ann. *Similes and Metaphors*. Mankato, MN: The Child's World, 2020.

Van Oosbree, Ruthie, and Lauren Kukla. *Free Verse Poems*. Minneapolis: Abdo Publishing, 2023.

NOTE TO EDUCATORS

Visit **www.focusreaders.com** to find lesson plans, activities, links, and other resources related to this title.

Index

C
computers, 9

D
date, 10, 27
decisions, 12
drawings, 19, 27

E
entries, 10, 12, 19–20, 25, 27
experimenting, 18

F
feelings, 6–7, 9, 12–13, 14, 20, 25–26

G
grammar, 17

M
memories, 12
mental health, 26
metaphors, 20

N
notebooks, 9

P
poetry, 19
prompts, 23–24, 27

S
schedule, 10
similes, 20
spelling, 17

T
thoughts, 9, 14, 17

Answer Key: 1. Answers will vary; **2.** Answers will vary; **3.** A; **4.** C; **5.** B; **6.** A